Using Leaves

Written by Jo Windsor

Look at the animals.
They are using leaves.
Animals use leaves
for different things.

2

3

This spider is using a leaf.
It is using a leaf to hide in.
The spider stays
inside the leaf.
It will come out
to catch its food.

4

spider

leaf

5

The bats are using
a leaf.
They are using the leaf
to keep away from the rain.
They can use the leaf
to sleep under.

bat

leaf

The ants are using leaves.
They take the leaves
back to the nest.
They are leafcutter ants.

leaf

ant

9

This bird is using leaves
to make a new nest.
The bird gets lots and lots
of leaves for its nest.
Now the bird can lay
its eggs.

leaves

bird

This orang-utan sleeps
in a tree.
It is using leaves
and branches.
It is using the leaves
and branches to make
a place to sleep.

branch

leaves

13

Index

Guide Notes

Title: Using Leaves
Stage: Early (4) – Green

Genre: Non-fiction
Approach: Guided Reading
Processes: Thinking Critically, Exploring Language, Processing Information
Written and Visual Focus: Photographs (static images), Labels, Index
Word Count: 149

THINKING CRITICALLY

(sample questions)
- Look at the title and read it to the children. Ask: "What do you think this book is going to tell us?"
- Ask the children what they know about animals that use leaves.
- Focus the children's attention on the index. Ask: "What are you going to find out about in this book?"
- If you want to find out about an orang-utan that uses leaves, what pages would you look on?
- If you want to find out about a spider that uses leaves, what page would you look on?
- Look at pages 4 and 5. Why do you think the spider is hiding?
- Look at pages 8 and 9. Why do you think these ants are called leafcutter ants?
- Look at pages 10 and 11. Why does this bird need a lot of leaves for its nest?
- What do you think is the difference between the leaf a spider uses and the leaf an orang-utan uses?

EXPLORING LANGUAGE

Terminology
Title, cover, photographs, author, photographers

Vocabulary
Interest words: leaves, leaf, leafcutter, branches, umbrella
High-frequency words: things, catch
Compound words: inside, away, leafcutter
Positional words: out, in, inside, out, under

Print Conventions
Capital letter for sentence beginnings, full stops, exclamation mark